THE RISEN STAR

Kgatlhiso Refilwe Matenge

Pharos Books

ISBN: 978-93-91103-31-6
eISBN: 978-93-91103-86-6

Publisher: Pharos Books (P) Ltd.
Plot No.-55, Main Mother Dairy Road
Pandav Nagar, East Delhi-110092
Phone: 011-40395855, +14049995474
WhatsApp: +91 8368220032
E-mail: sales@pharosbooks.in
Website: www.pharosbooks.in
Edition: 2021

The Risen Star
Author: Kgatlhiso Refilwe Matenge

Contents

Acknowledgements

I would like to thank my friends, family and loved ones for the motivation and support all throughout. Mostly God for imparting such a gift on me. Also Show Casing Talents for giving me such a platform.

Introduction

The *Risen Star* is a combination of poems touching different aspects of life. It's a life journey and experience written in a poetic form. It's also healing and a little redemption in some way. Fun and exciting moments all together.

About The Author

Kgatlhiso Refilwe Matenge is a 20 year old young woman from Kanye and the only child of her parents. Currently she is awaiting to pursue her studies at the University of Botswana

The Hatchet

WHY, WHY, WHY?
Have you destroyed my joy?
You gave me harsh beating
As a death penalty to take me to my fate

A fallen star
Heart torn apart
My thoughts flowing like a river
As I compete with my inner self.
You were ready to avenge on me
Absolute revenge

A voice of agony screamed out
There came various sounds
As if they are about to collide
I was in complete confusion

Having no direction to look at
Poor me!

I felt like dying
As you overweighed me
I was left there in suspense
But sorry
It's your end
Goodbye my painful past
Your death sentence is out.

Listen

There came sounds roaring like a lion
I could hear them all over.
I did not know which one to follow
As they were in unison

They were the voices of people
Ordering me around
As if I'm their little puppet
Ruling me over

I resisted the calling
As I felt a deep sound coming from within
Sadly I was alone at the crossroad
But still I had to find my own
Listen to this bold voice
Here are my sayings:
"My time has come"

For dreams to be heard and not to be pushed aside
Be turned to those of others'
But to become of my own.

Darkness

All alone in a dungeon
As hallow as a drum
Everything completely dark
Emptiness filled me

My dreams were shattered
My visions were unclear
Everything was blurring
I became low spirited

Death came in to flee me away
To set me free from all bounds
If only I knew my melancholy will end
As light brightens up
To chase away the temporal darkness

I rose up
I fought like a warrior
As my liberation meant a lot to me

Happiness filled up the deep hole.

Resentment

Nothing is to be compared to this feeling
Where nobody cares
Not even a little inch about how you feel
Tearing you apart

All eyes staring at you
Ready to judge you
Irreversible words sounding
All to weaken you
Bringing regrets

People pushing you aside
As you followed your own voice
Making you feel bad
Your world being turned upside down
As suddenly all seem to be crashing you down

Only death was your permit out
As it gave you privilege to disappear
To never feel the brutal pains
Bought into your life.

Nature

The motherland God has created
A world full of adventures
Beauty is shown in all places
A true land of beauty

Mountains high to climb
Oceans flowing down
Streams and rivers filled with water
Vegetation blooming out
Scenic beauty revealed

Birds flying above
Making a unison rhythm
They remind me of angels praising God
Roaring sounds of animals being heard all over
Sounding like a trumpet that will sound in all
Corners of the earth during Rapture

Pans, deltas and ponds giving out their
Sheering beauty
To capture the souls of many
Minerals exposed
The earth casing out its beauty

Stars shinning above
They keep on twinkling
The sun that lightens the day
Rains that fill the earth with blessing
Nature revealing itself
The greatest vessel ever made
As a resemblance of God
To take control over nature
Authority being emphasized

Nature gives in like a locus flower
Showers love like a rose
Enlightens like a petunia
Strengthens like an aloe plant

With thorns that hardens
To tell nature that it can survive.

Sun Rise

A morning star
As bright as a new penny
Rising in the morning
Up there
To lighten up the day

Birds flying above
Children making noises
Adults making praises
Voices being heard all over
Praising the new day

You give us hope
By rising above the sky
A new chapter to write about
New beginnings indeed

Laughter and joy
Is what you bring to the world
To make us forget the darkness we have endured
To keep us at ease for a while

For you live on longer than the night
Even deep in the souls you enlighten us
Your rule over us will never end.

Death

Where are you from?
Why did you choose to dwell in our midst?

Who gave you the keys to our lives?
For you suddenly entered and swept us all

You never cared whom you took away
For the young and the old are the same to you
You are so cruel
Each house is your dwelling place
There is no place other than our homes

You leave us defenseless
We have no direction to look at
You left some as orphans with no one to fend for them
Some as widows and widowers with no companions

Others without their loved ones
You take people to their early graves
Leaving the rest in dismay
In confusion of whom you are going to take next
Please go and find a place elsewhere
For you living amongst us brings a lot of pain
Go! and forever this time.

Hate

Where are you from?
What made you to hold us in captive of your territory?
You made us your descendants
A true version of being servants

You only chose the hearts of men
You made them despise one another
Men curse each other
Not wishing each other well
Just like twitter you have followers

Even the young ones you have sowed your seeds on them
they envy each other
They deeply despise one another
You made them think it is the only way to live
As you dwelled in their midst at a tender age

You walk with pride as if you own the world
Everywhere you mark your territory
Indeed you did win over this world
For you hover at all places
It's time to let you go
We no longer require your services.

Lover

You sparkle on like a diamond
My heart pounds as if it could break my rib cage
At the sound of your name
I feel exhilarated

You are my knight armour
My ride and die
I wish I could ride along with you in a chariot
Songs of love sounding from all corners
Dancing like the ballet people
To the beat of the music

My Prince charming
My Romeo
My World

It pleases me to be your Juliet
The king of my palace
Words can never describe my love for you
Even artists cannot sing it

Poets cannot express it
Storytellers cannot tell tales about it
Architects cannot draw it
Builders cannot build it
I love you more than the expressible feelings.

Women

Wonderfully and fearfully made
To become the mother of the motherless

A tower of strength
A comforter
A guide to the lost sheep

She shields at her bosom
She brings joy to the low spirited
She brightens the darkened souls

A mother of all nations
A pain barrier
As strong as Hercules
She still rises

Harsh storms pass by her
The stormy waters like that of the disciples of Jesus
She makes them come still
Reminding me of Jesus

She expresses faith from deep within
She is bold as a lioness
I remember back then about the past strong women
Martha, Mary, Esther and other women

Behold he said, "Women! Do not weep for me; weep for yourselves and your own children."

Indeed she has faith
She does not fear bearing pain
Weeping for a child she bore
As she remembers the pain of labour
The seed of her womb

She remembered Jesus at the grave
As she does for her children at their weakest points
She becomes their hope
Favour is her name
Integrity is her foot steps
Confidence is her make up

Beauty is her art.

Door Bells

Knock, knock!
Who's there?
It is me
Who?
Reality
Come in, please

Take a seat
Thank you
How may I help you?

I am here to offer you some advice
Advise about what?
Life in general
I beg to leave now
Bye!

Another door bell
"I am back again"
What more do you want?
I have words to fully say to you
I am all ears

A little remorse back
I was young, waiting to see the world
Little did I know, I was just as close to seeing it

There came in fear
Of how I am going to deal with the world
To experience its sour taste
To feel its ups and downs
To walk through its deepest valley
To hear its roars

There I was
Feeling the pressure of the lava
Thoughts pouring out like lava from a magma chamber
To bring about something
Only if I knew

Life was difficult
I could have reversed me
To become young again
Poor me!
That is impossible

I'm sorry
I have to face reality
Live the moment
Revive the me
Prepare for eternity

For tomorrow is not promised
Goodbye!

Negligence

At a young tender age
Hardships passed by you
You questioned yourself:
"Why me?"
It's a pity you did not have all the answers

You laid there helpless
The ones to fend for you were no more
They have all left
The pestilence of the night

Arrows fleeing by day
As lonely as the Artic sea
All by yourself

The world watched you sob
As mournful as the grave
No one was there for you
If only they knew it was for some time
Your pain would soon turn into joy

Hang in there little one
You are not alone

The one above is watching over you
The best is yet to come
Your star is about to shine brightly
The darkness will soon turn into light.

Street Child

Listen to the voice of a little child
Crying in the wilderness
As she cries tears of pain
With no one to give her comfort
With no place to call home
With no one to call mum or dad

The streets are her only place of comfort
A place to call home
She has to struggle for food
Her bed of sorrow and discomfort
Are the scrubbed boxes and dustbins

The scorching sun and harsh storms
She has to face daily
She cannot run away from them because
She has nowhere to run to
Listen to her agony as she cries
"I am cursed." She says
I am useless

She feels like dying naturally
Inside she is completely dead
She finds no happiness
Her world is crumbling down
Only ill fate departs her from anguish
She could feel that she has completely won
Lord have mercy
Help her rejuvenate life again

She is a blessing
It does not matter where she lives
Let her find relief
May she find confidence in herself
That is her daily prayer.

Hardship

At a young tender age
My beloved 18 year old self
A knock off hit me
Life unveiling itself

I asked myself many questions
Weeping was my daily bread
The only place of comfort became a place of horror Isolated!
That alone separated her from the rest

She could go on many days without eating
Harsh words were her daily bread
Someone to keep her at their bosom

Left her there all alone
To deal with the harsh beatings of this world
Hang in there baby girl
Your God is watching
He will secure you a place of refuge

There shall sorrow ever befall on you
A place of divine peace
Like an eagle you will rise
Take a few steps forward
Your joy is yet to come
In the matter of me.

Flames

You were down
I picked you up
As a lost sheep in wander
I brought you back
You were cold
I gave you warmth

I set on the fire for you
I loved you as my own
You just watched me
All you saw was a fool

You were falling
I stretched my arms to reach you
You walked away
Leaving me all alone

You were drowning
I jumped in the waters to get you off
You let me drown
You watched me die
Dying for love.

Farewell

I never hoped to bid you farewell
Moreover to say my final goodbye
You left suddenly
All the hopes were crushed down
When you left and said goodbye

You could have let me know of your departure
As I take time to prepare
To let you go

Your departure was so sudden
Too bad I cannot reverse time

As I saw that little casket
I knew it was the end
I was given the platform to relentlessly talk
about you I ran out of words

Lacking your presence torn me apart
That moment I saw the coffin go down
My world trembled
As I paid off my last respects

It was saddening
As I silently let you at your resting place
May you find rest
Until we meet again
Dedicated to my departed friend.

Goodbye Alphabet

Although we are parting ways
Because we have reached the end
Continue with that same love
Don't break the bond

Even when we may never meet again like this
Fate will bring us together again
God is there for us
Hold onto him

Imagine about the future
Journey to it has began
Keep on moving
Life is awaiting on you all

Mountains are there for us to climb
New chapters to start kick
Obeying the ticking of time
Power exerted on us

Quit worrying about your failures
Redeeem the time at hand
Start believing in yourself
Time itself will do its course
Until you reach your destiny
Victoriously we will shout

We will run with gratitude
Xalting the victory
Yes times will be rough but
Zealously run to fetch the baton and finish off the race.

Remedy

When you call I will be there
When you cry I will wipe away the tears
When you fall I will catch you
When you are down I will pick you up
When you are joyful I will rejoice with you

No matter how far I will be
Distance is not a problem
I could travel miles to reach for you

Even if it means travelling through the darkness
For you will I will take the sacrifice
Fear not
I will be with you all the way

I will be your shepherd
Even in the darkest valley
Call on me
I will be your remedy.

"Salt of The Earth "

I said to myself
"Dineo! You are the salt of the earth
Being the white elephant
You have always been

It's time!
You turn over a new leaf
It's no use being a rough diamond
Stand strong
Fight the woes

Be yourself!
Be cautious of time
Be as useful as a cow
Beware!

Time is not at hand
Be the Good Samaritan
You have always been

Don't dim that light
As bright as a new shilling
Keep it on

Don't extinct the charisma."

Be My Valentine

A feather in one's cap
Was the day
I final set my eyes on you
Was it on cards?

It seemed impossible
You being mine
For it was love
At first sight

I was in seventh heaven
When you finally became mine I kept on mingling

Walking on the air
As pleased as a punch
I could not wait

For a life
Coated with love
In desolate places

Parched!
Did I never know
That one day
I will finally flee
Into the arms of an angel

Then I shall be at the
Garden of Eden

Why did it take long?
For the maker of all
to unite us
But finally destiny

Played the role
My heart pleas
The mouth sings
"Be my valentine."

Let us ride together
Through thick and thin
Pain
Happiness

But above all
In everything
Love is as rare as a blue rose
But where I found love

It is in the limited
Of all places
In my solidity

You came in
Cleared all the speculations
Now I cannot wait
For a life time
With you

Where I can finally
Look you in the eyes
And say "you are the best thing
That has ever happened to me."

As I lie in your arms
Close my eyes
At your bosom
Say my last love you
And sleep forever.

The Good Fight

As numerous as the sands
Upon the ocean shore
Lassitude
Struggles
Difficulties
Were as voluminous

To move heaven and earth
Even in tuber lance
In invincibility

Discouraged
Down cast
Disgruntled, deeply
As tears flooded

All dubious
Momentarily?
Yes!
Throw in the sponge?

Neither here nor there
But it being
The only option
As firm as Rocky Mountains
Rosen up

Stuck in muddy clays Deep oceanic waves
All revering

Kept the ball rolling
Rising from the cinerary
Fought audaciously
Knowingly
Had an axe to grind
Than to bite the dust
As keen as mustard
Ready than ever
To fight

THE GOOD FIGHT.

Pearls Before Swine

As hearty as an oak
Swore
All ones eggs in one basket
For those that mattered

Jumping the gun
Entirely for them
As hasty as a gun
Bestowing all odds

Casting pearls before swine
Off one's own bat
Master planning
The events of life
Actually not mine

A little bit of gratitude?
Oh, no!
Labour was all in vain
The necessity in the eyes

Became pellucid
All was opprobrium
After realising

Too much of one thing
As powerless as an infant
Everything was left as it is.

www.ingramcontent.com/pod-product-compliance
Lightning Source LLC
LaVergne TN
LVHW100339181026
850499LV00039B/1137
9789391103316